Voices From The Past ★ ★ ★ ★ ★ ★ ★ ★ ★ ★ ★

WAR OF 1812

KATHLYN GAY   MARTIN GAY

Twenty-First Century Books
A Division of Henry Holt and Company
New York

Twenty-First Century Books
A Division of Henry Holt and Company, Inc.
115 West 18th Street
New York, NY 10011

Henry Holt® and colophon are trademarks of
Henry Holt and Company, Inc.
Publishers since 1866

Published in Canada by Fitzhenry & Whiteside Ltd.
195 Allstate Parkway, Markham, Ontario L3R 4T8

Library of Congress Cataloging-in-Publication Data
Gay, Kathlyn.
War of 1812 / Kathlyn Gay and Martin Gay. — 1st ed.
p. cm. — (Voices from the past)
Includes bibliographical references (p.) and index.
1. United States—History—War of 1812—Juvenile literature.
[1. United States—History—War of 1812.] I. Gay, Martin, 1950- .
II. Title. III. Series: Gay, Kathlyn. Voices from the past.
E354.G39 1995   95–13417
973.5'2—dc20   CIP
                                                            AC

ISBN 0–8050–2846–3
First Edition 1995

Printed in the United States of America
All first editions are printed on acid-free paper ∞.
10 9 8 7 6 5 4 3 2 1

Map by Vantage Art, Inc.
Cover design by Karen Quigley
Interior design by Kelly Soong

Cover: *Battle Of North Point* by Don Troiani
Photograph courtesy of Historical Art Prints, Southbury, CT.

Photo credits
pp. 9, 24, 29: U.S. Army Center of Military History; pp. 10, 14, 32, 52: The Bettmann
Archive; p. 12: Delaware Art Museum, Wilmington/Louisa du Pont Copeland
Memorial Fund, 1951; pp. 16, 19, 44, 55: North Wind Picture Archives; pp. 27, 57:
The Granger Collection; p. 36: Buffalo and Erie County Historical Society; p. 39:
Anne S. K. Brown Military Collection, Brown University Library; p. 47: Smithsonian
Institution NMAH; p. 49: Picture Collection, The Branch Libraries, The New York
Public Library.

Contents

Acknowledgments

Some of the research for this series depended upon the special efforts of Dean Hamilton, who spent many hours locating primary source materials and other references on America's wars and sorting out appropriate stories among the many personal accounts available. Especially helpful was his work at the archival library of the University of South Florida at Tampa, researching for Spanish-American War and Civil War narratives. For the *World War I* title in this series, Dean also applied his special talents interviewing several of the few remaining veterans of WW I, obtaining their highly personal recollections, which the veterans allowed us to include. Thanks, Dean.

In addition, we would like to thank Lt. Col. (retired) John McGarrahan for locating narratives about personal experiences in the War of 1812, available in the archives at the Lilly Library, Indiana University, Bloomington, Indiana. We also thank Douglas Gay for obtaining narratives on the battle of Tippecanoe at the Tippecanoe County Historical Association in Lafayette, Indiana. Portions of these accounts are included in the *War of 1812* title in this series.

—*Kathlyn Gay and Martin Gay*

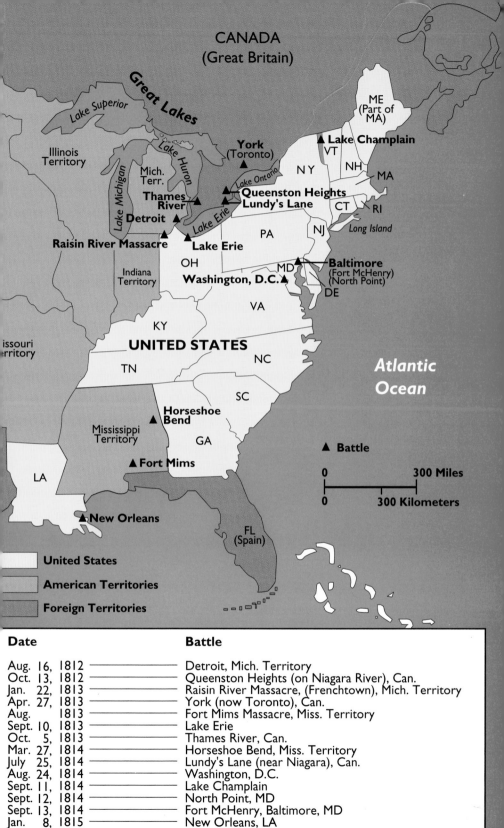

CANADA
(Great Britain)

Great Lakes

Lake Superior

Illinois
Territory

Lake Michigan

Lake Huron

Mich.
Terr.

▲ York
(Toronto)

ME
(Part of
MA)

▲ Lake Champlain
VT

Lake Ontario

NY

NH

MA

Queenston Heights
Lundy's Lane

CT

RI

Thames
River

Detroit ▲

Lake Erie

▲ Raisin River Massacre ▲

▲ Lake Erie

OH

PA

NJ

Long Island

MD ▲

Baltimore
(Fort McHenry)
(North Point)

Indiana
Territory

Washington, D.C. ▲

DE

issouri
rritory

KY

VA

UNITED STATES

TN

NC

SC

Mississippi
Territory

▲ Horseshoe
Bend

GA

▲ Fort Mims

▲ Battle

LA

0   300 Miles

0   300 Kilometers

▲ New Orleans

FL
(Spain)

Atlantic
Ocean

United States

American Territories

Foreign Territories

Date		Battle
Aug. 16, 1812	———	Detroit, Mich. Territory
Oct. 13, 1812	———	Queenston Heights (on Niagara River), Can.
Jan. 22, 1813	———	Raisin River Massacre, (Frenchtown), Mich. Territory
Apr. 27, 1813	———	York (now Toronto), Can.
Aug. 1813	———	Fort Mims Massacre, Miss. Territory
Sept. 10, 1813	———	Lake Erie
Oct. 5, 1813	———	Thames River, Can.
Mar. 27, 1814	———	Horseshoe Bend, Miss. Territory
July 25, 1814	———	Lundy's Lane (near Niagara), Can.
Aug. 24, 1814	———	Washington, D.C.
Sept. 11, 1814	———	Lake Champlain
Sept. 12, 1814	———	North Point, MD
Sept. 13, 1814	———	Fort McHenry, Baltimore, MD
Jan. 8, 1815	———	New Orleans, LA

One

THE PRELUDE TO WAR

In the years following the Revolutionary War, the United States as a young republic faced difficulties trying to guarantee protection for some of its citizens. Foreign warships searching for deserters from their armies and navies frequently attacked American ships on the high seas; Americans were taken from their ships and forced to serve with a foreign military.

There was also conflict on land. On the western frontier, various Indian nations claimed territory, and some tribes were increasingly hostile to the growing presence of American settlers. Even before the Revolutionary War ended, some Native Americans in the North and West had joined the British side, hoping to force out settlers who were taking their land and destroying their way of life. With the defeat of the British army, the native people had to deal with the government of the United States, which refused to treat them as equals.

Yet Native Americans never conceded defeat. They continued to operate as free and independent nations, and tribes banded together to fight their common foe. There were continual uprisings and attacks throughout the frontier as hundreds of thousands of pioneers moved from the East to Kentucky, Tennessee, and the Northwest Territory, which included the state of Ohio and the territories of Michigan, Illinois, and Indiana.

President George Washington sent the army to quell the problem in the newly settled regions of New York and the Ohio Valley, but the soldiers were not well trained. They suffered some serious defeats at the hands of Indian warriors who had the help of their old ally, the British. Indian Agent Jacob Varnum in the Sandusky, Ohio, trading post noted, "As was [the British] custom, immense quantities of goods were . . . distributed among the Indians with the view of securing their allegiance and aid to butcher the women and children on the frontier."[1]

A NEW APPROACH

General "Mad Anthony" Wayne tried to stop the Indians' marauding in the Northwest Territory. He spent a full year drilling and training his men into a crack fighting unit. When the time came to take on the proud forces of Shawnee, Miami, Potawatomi, and Chippewa led by Little Turtle in the Ohio River Valley, General Wayne was ready.

Little Turtle knew this and told the other chiefs, "We have beaten the enemy twice under different commanders. . . . The Americans are now led by a chief who never sleeps."[2] Little Turtle advised the tribal chiefs to negotiate an honorable peace. But he was ignored, and a less experienced chief led the Indian fighters into a historic defeat at Fallen Timbers, near present-day Toledo, Ohio.

The combined tribes then agreed in 1795 to meet at Fort Greenville, Ohio, where a treaty was signed with American representatives. In return for a payment of $10,000 per year, the tribes gave up their lands in Ohio and Indiana, and the Northwest Territory was opened for settlement. The Treaty of Greenville finally ended nearly two

*The Indians were defeated by General Anthony Wayne at
the Battle of Fallen Timbers in August 1794.*

decades of fighting in what some have called the last phase
of the War of Independence.

TECUMSEH AND THE SHAWNEE PROPHET

The leader of the Shawnee at the Battle of Fallen Timbers
was Tecumseh, a proud and intelligent leader who refused to
take part in the treaty signing at Greenville. Tecumseh had
been educated in world history and the classics by a young
settler, Rebecca Galloway, who was well-read even at ten years
old. He came to respect and love the blond, blue-eyed girl.
When she was sixteen, he asked her to marry him. She insist-
ed that he begin to live as the whites did, and Tecumseh said

In the Treaty of Greenville, the Indians agreed to give up much of their land in southern Ohio.

he would consider this until the next moon. A month later, he returned with his answer: he could never abandon his duty and his people. Tecumseh would never see Rebecca again.

For ten years after the Battle of Fallen Timbers, Tecumseh and his younger brother, Laulewasika, organized the surrounding tribes into a confederation, or union. The tribes agreed to oppose any more land sales to the American settlers.

During this time, Laulewasika took the name Tenskwatawa (meaning "the open door"). People called him The Prophet because he would go into trances, see visions, and then predict coming events. After coming out of a trance one day, he said he had received a message from the "other side" telling him to protect the Shawnee way of life and the land of their ancestors.

Although Tenskwatawa as a religious leader built the morale of his people, Tecumseh was the stronger of the two brothers and was highly respected for his leadership. Together they were an effective team. They established their base at Prophet's Town along the Tippecanoe River in Indiana Territory and directed raids and mischief against the whites between 1805 and 1811.

The governor of the territory, General William Henry Harrison, became increasingly alarmed at Tecumseh's power. By 1809, Prophet's Town was overflowing with Wyandots, Delawares, Shawnee, Ojibwas, Kickapoos, and Ottawas who had agreed to keep settlers out of the territory. Harrison wrote that Tecumseh was "one of those uncommon geniuses" because of his ability to unite the people, and that "if it were not for the vicinity of the United States, he would perhaps be the founder of an Empire that would rival in glory Mexico or Peru."[3]

Harrison invited Tecumseh for a meeting. The Shawnee leader arrived with 400 warriors at Vincennes in August of 1810. Governor Harrison asked Tecumseh to take a seat with territory officials, saying it was the wish of the "Great Father, the President of the United States, that you do so." Tecumseh instead laid himself on the bare earth and replied, "My Father—The Sun is my father, the Earth is my mother—and on her bosom I will recline!"[4]

Tecumseh and Harrison reached no understanding at the Vincennes meeting. Clearly, Tecumseh and his people would not bow to the authority of the American officials. In fact, by 1811, Harrison believed Tecumseh and his followers would soon start a war. So he called for regular army troops to reinforce the militia in Indiana Territory and to help build a fort, called Fort Harrison.

Tecumseh was a strong unifying force among the Indian tribes.
He is shown here at a meeting with General William Henry Harrison,
governor of the Indiana Territory.

HARRISON'S OPPORTUNITY

Not long after reinforcements arrived, General Harrison
learned that Tecumseh was traveling around the southern
United States, trying to convince the various tribes to join his
union. With Tecumseh gone, the general decided to strike.
He led a force of about 1,000 men to the region just west of
Prophet's Town, near the Tippecanoe River.

The Prophet was in charge while Tecumseh was away. Tecumseh had warned his brother not to confront the soldiers, but The Prophet went his own way. He told his warriors that the white men's bullets could not hit them and that if the warriors screamed, the American soldiers would run. At the same time, The Prophet sent some of his men to Harrison. According to Shabonee, a Potawatomi chief who was there, the messengers reported that "the Indians were all peaceable . . . they did not want to fight." The messenger told Harrison to "lie down and sleep," and the Indians would meet "with their white brothers in the morning and bury the hatchet."[5]

The Prophet, however, was preparing to attack. So was Harrison. John Tipton, a young ensign in the militia known as the Harrison County Yellow Jackets, recorded in his journal on November 6, 1811:

> we moved Earley a Scout Sent out they Came back had seed indian Sine we marched as usuel till 12 our Spies Caught four horses and Seed Some indians found we ware near the Celebrated Prophets town we formd in order for Battle marched 2 miles then formd the line of Battle we marchd in 5 lines to the above town and Surrounded it the[y] met us Pled for Peace the[y] Said the[y] would give us Satisfaction in the morning all the time we ware there they kept hallowing[6]

The next day was "thirsday the 7," and Tipton reported that the Shawnee kept their promise:

> a blood Combat took Plaice at Precisely 15 minutes before five in the morning which lasted 2 hours and 20 minuts of a Continewel firing while maney times mixd among the indians So that we Could not tell them indians and our men

General Harrison (far left) defeated the Indians under
Tecumseh's brother, known as The Prophet, at the
Battle of Tippecanoe in November 1811. As a result, a number
of tribes fought for the British in the following War of 1812.

apart   they kept up a firing on three sides of us . . . our men
fought brave . . . we maid a Charge and Drove them out of
our timber across the Prarie   our Losst in killed and
wounded was 179 and theirs graiter than ours.[7]

Many historians say that this now famous Battle of
Tippecanoe was really the beginning of the major war to
come.

Two

TROUBLED WATERS

The problems of the young country were not confined to the western frontier. Merchants and seamen of New England towns who made their living by trading goods and services with European markets were in an uproar. England and France had been at war since 1793, and in order to punish their enemy, the British passed laws banning trade with France. American traders had been doing a brisk business with both of the combatants, and they were incensed by the British tactics. After all, hadn't they just won a war to eliminate the oppressive hand of the English king from their lives?

When the Americans ignored the orders and continued their trade with France and its colonies throughout the world, the mighty British navy began to seize American merchant ships. An anonymous teenage sailor aboard an American vessel that was chased for fourteen hours described what it was like just before capture by a British brig (a type of warship):

> The brig kept up a steady fire upon us.... At half past 6, the enemy was near enough to pour into us, volley after volley, of musketry. Our little skipper seemed to be in his glory; he ordered all but a few men to go below, ... but did

me the high honor to select me as one of the few to keep the deck,—a distinction for which, I am afraid, I was not very grateful.

Our sails and rigging were completely cut by the musketry, but not a man was hurt....At 7 o'clock, all hope of escape departed from the captain. He mounted up into the main rigging, and hailing the brig, announced our surrender.[1]

Hundreds of ships were taken in this manner, prompting some Americans to call for war with Britain. However, American officials tried to maintain peace and sent John Jay, the first chief justice of the U.S. Supreme Court, to negotiate a treaty with the British. The British eventually signed the Jay Treaty in 1794, but terms of the treaty called for the United States to cut off trade with France. Many Americans were furi-

British ships would frequently attempt to capture American merchant vessels.

ous, accusing Chief Justice Jay of betraying the United States. Then new fighting between France and England erupted in 1803, and the Jay Treaty expired soon after, which led to almost intolerable British harassment of American vessels.

MORE TROUBLE BETWEEN FRANCE AND ENGLAND

During the early 1800s, the successes of the French leader Napoleon Bonaparte made his country the undisputed victor throughout the European continent. But Napoleon was unable to invade England because of British mastery of the seas. So he ordered a blockade of the British Isles. No ships would be allowed to trade with France's enemy.

In retaliation, the British government issued orders in council commanding the Royal Navy once again to seize any ship caught trading with France. The law also ordered the navy to impress, or take by force, any sailors from foreign ships who they suspected were deserters. Many British sailors deserted because of terrible conditions on board their ships.

When the British stopped U.S. ships and inspected them, they took, along with deserters, many American sailors, insisting they were not U.S. citizens. The Americans were then forced to serve on British vessels. James M'Lean of Connecticut, a young man who had gone to sea on a merchant ship at the age of ten, described what happened to him after leaving a port in Grenada during the early 1800s:

> We had no sooner let go our anchor, than an English Man of War's boat, came on board and [im]pressed me and two more of the Seamen, and carried us on . . . [a] 50 gun ship, commanded by John Dilks, who immediately asked me for my protection [identification]. I immediately shewed him one from a Notary Public in New York. . . . He replied, "I could get one, if I was in America, for half a crown, as good

as that." He further said, "it is of no use for you to pretend that you are an American, for you was born in Scotland."[2]

For the next few years, M'Lean was forced to serve on British ships. But one day, while in a London port, he escaped and signed on with an American merchant ship, where he served for more than a year. Then, during a storm, his ship was forced to go to England again. M'Lean reported in his journal:

> While we lay there, I went on shore for water; while watering, an [English] officer came down to the boat, with a guard of soldiers, and asked me "what countryman I was." I answered, an American. He said "that I must go with him;" upon which he put me into the guard house, and ordered the guard to take good care of me, as he presumed I was a deserter from the navy.[3]

Again M'Lean was impressed, and he spent another decade or so on British frigates. The injustices suffered by many sailors like M'Lean led some U.S. congressmen, who were known as War Hawks, to become more and more vocal in their demands to go to war against England.

Yet very little preparation had been made for waging a real war. The new president, James Madison, had opted to keep only a small naval fleet, and there was no major support in the states to pay for an army large enough to do an effective job on the land. Thus the government decided to rely on short-term enlistees and the state militia should the need for troops arise.

AN OPPORTUNITY FOR EXPANSION

The prospect of going to war was highly controversial, however. New England merchants were still reaping profits from

The British forced many Americans to serve on British ships.
This injustice was one of the causes behind the War of 1812.

their trade with countries in Europe and the Caribbean. And where they could get away with it, smuggling goods into England and France could pay very well. Their representatives in Congress, the Federalists, saw war with England as a foolish step; it would cause loss of trade routes, disrupt normal society, and cost a lot of money. Since the Federalists in Congress had the most power, they were able to slow the preparations for fighting.

The War Hawks, however, kept up the pressure. They saw advantages in going to war. In their view, the "Indian problem" in the West and South could finally be addressed. As one newspaper editorial said, "The blood of our fellow-citizens murdered on the Wabash by British intrigue calls aloud for vengeance."[4]

War Hawks also believed that with a sufficient force of soldiers, land in Canada could be captured, or at the very least, the Canadian and British support of the tribes could finally be ended. If the United States could add to its territory under the pretext of maintaining security, all the better. Many thought that Canada would immediately side with the United States once Canadians were "liberated" in a war effort.

Three

DECLARATION OF WAR

In 1811, both houses of the U.S. Congress were controlled by Democratic-Republican War Hawks, including members from the South and West who were fearful of more and more Indian attacks. Even though the country was not prepared, President Madison had to convene the Congress in a special session in November of that year to consider an armed response to England's policies.

For weeks, members of Congress argued back and forth about the next move that should be made. Some congressmen advocated declaring war against Britain and France, as both countries had taken American ships and caused great hardship to American sailors and merchants.

In the end, the debate centered on Great Britain and its abuse of American merchantmen and naval vessels. The British took twice as many merchantmen as the French did—about 1,000 American seamen a year were impressed by the British prior to 1812.

A NEEDLESS WAR?

U.S. government officials demanded that England overturn its orders that required all trade with Europe to go through a British port. When no response came from England, the U.S.

Congress voted for war. President Madison signed the declaration on June 18, 1812.

Ironically, British government officials had also been arguing among themselves about the orders. Loss of trade with the former colonies was harmful to many English merchants. Then Britain's prime minister, who supported the orders, was shot in an assassination attempt. As a result, the government policy weakened, and the orders were rescinded on June 16, 1812, two days before the American declaration of war.

If the "reason" for the war was gone, why did the U.S. Congress decide to fight anyway? Because they didn't know that the British had ended the orders in council. News at that time took weeks to travel from the British Isles, across the Atlantic Ocean, to the shores of America. Once the declaration of war was made, there was no turning back.

BALTIMORE RIOTS

Federalist politicians spoke out against taking up arms. A widely circulated pamphlet of the time criticized the Democratic-Republicans for starting a war they were ill prepared to fight, especially one that seemed calculated only to invade the Canadian lands to the north. "How will war upon the land protect commerce upon the seas?" was one question the pamphlet asked. The author asserted that the United States was "rushing into difficulties, with little calculation about the means, and little concern about the consequences. . . . Let us not be deceived, a war of invasion may invite a retort of invasion."[1]

The emotional response of many citizens to their government's declaration of war carried the day. Anyone who questioned the reasoning behind the war preparations was called a traitor, a Tory, and a friend of England. Newspaper editorials threatened harsh treatment for those who didn't support the effort. "The war will separate the partisans of England from the honest federalists & *Tar* & *Feathers* will cure their penchant for our enemy," one editorial warned.[2]

The threats became real in Baltimore just days after war was declared. A Federalist newspaper had published an editorial that was very critical of the Democratic-Republicans, accusing them of ignoring the basic rights of those holding a minority opinion. A drunken mob soon gathered at the paper's office on Gay Street, and in a short time they had destroyed the building and its contents. When a law officer was asked to stop the mayhem, he replied that the publisher was "a rascal" and the crowd "ought to put a rope around his neck, and draw him out of town, then hang him on the first tree they came to."[3]

Two weeks later, the Federalist paper was published again, this time secretly in Georgetown, in Washington, D.C. It was brought into Baltimore for distribution. Incensed that the publishers would once more defy the supporters of war, a drunken crowd surrounded a house where the editor and about two dozen Federalists had gathered. The mob threatened to kill the Federalists and even brought in a cannon aimed at the front door. Reluctantly the authorities intervened to take the Federalists to jail for their own protection. The mob surrounded the Federalists, screaming and throwing cobblestones at them until they were inside the jail.

The next day, the hateful crowd milled around the jail yard into the evening hours, then finally pushed through the doors and found the Federalists. A few escaped in the darkness, but most were beaten until they could no longer move. They were then piled in a heap outside the jail, where they were stabbed and beaten repeatedly. Some died. One eyewitness noted, "Such expressions as these were current—'We'll root out the damn'd tories.' 'We'll drink their blood.' 'We'll eat their hearts.'"[4]

Though the war fever was high, it was not a simple task to put enough fighters into the battlefield. Congress did not authorize the recruitment of a large force until after war was declared, and then there was not enough money to pay recruits a decent wage, let alone a bonus for enlisting. Most men joined their state militias, where they were usually assured that they would not have to leave their homes.

As in the Revolutionary War, some women also served, disguising themselves as men and signing on with a ship's

Some women aided U.S. forces during the war.
Here, a woman supplies hot cannonballs to the artillery.

crew or with land forces. Still, the army only numbered 7,000 and the navy included only a few ships.

Luckily the enemy was occupied in a war with France. In addition, supply lines to support an army at war against the United States were long and hazardous. Thus Americans had a little time to prepare before they were really tested. However, they needed more than time, because the federal government could not supply its forces adequately. An Ohio volunteer waiting to be sent north to fight in Canada described the miserable life at camp:

> Our sufferings at this place have been greater than if we had been in a severe battle: more than one hundred lives have been lost owing to our bad accommodations! The sufferings of about three hundred sick at this time, which are exposed to the cold ground, and deprived of nourishment, are suffi-cient proofs of our wretched condition!—The camp has become a loathsome place: The hope of being one day relieved from these unnecessary sufferings affords some relief.—We received this evening a supply of flour and have been delivered from a state of starvation—it being Christmas eve.[5]

Four

WAR IN THE WEST

The first offensive of the war was against Canada in the Great Lakes region, where it was assumed the enemy was most vulnerable. Almost twice as many U.S. citizens as Canadians and other British allies lived in the area. Brigadier General William Hull, the fifty-nine-year-old governor of the Michigan Territory, was chosen to lead the attack.

Hull had seen honorable service in the Revolutionary War but had retired from active duty. Although he had suffered a stroke and his health had deteriorated, he expected to serve the nation well. This was clear in a letter written May 12, 1812, to Charles Scott, his old commander in the Revolution:

> Altho' too advanced in years, I am again entering on a military life. I only hope, I may be useful to my country. It inspires me with great confidence, and it is a source of great satisfaction to me, to witness the spirit of my Countrymen nearest the scene where I shall probably be called to act.[1]

Even before the declaration of war, Hull was given orders to assemble 2,000 troops in Ohio to prepare for a march to Detroit. There, it was hoped, such a large show of strength would convince the Canadians, the British, and their Indian allies to abandon the area around Lakes Huron and Erie. The only regions of any importance to the United States in vast Canada were those that could be reached by water. That is where the settlers were, and that is how travel and trade were accomplished.

THE TREK INTO THE FRONTIER

Among Hull's troops who prepared to march was Lieutenant Josiah Bacon. His wife, Lydia, accompanied him, since families often went with officers on the long treks, waiting in towns and villages when the men had to go into combat. Lydia kept a record of her journey along the rough trail Hull was forging into hostile territory and wrote letters to her mother and sister in Boston.

In one entry written in August 1812, Lydia described

This 1813 cartoon makes fun of the fact that a soldier going to the front was often accompanied by his entire family.

boarding a small ship sent to transport the sick and the baggage and other supplies of the officers. "We embarked, & enjoyed the sail very much, after riding Horseback nearly 600 miles & sleeping on the ground 50 nights. We were in high spirits." But very soon, a large British ship came into view and hailed them to surrender. "The sails was lowered & the English Capt with his Men jumped on board deligh'ed with their prieze, most of the Hospital stores were on board & all the Officers baggage."[2]

Also on board was enough information to give British Major General Isaac Brock a good idea of what Hull was planning to do at Detroit. Brock later said, "Till I received these letters, I had no idea General Hull was advancing with so large a force."[3] This information allowed Brock and his new ally, the great Shawnee chief Tecumseh, to create a daring plan to capture Fort Detroit.

Tecumseh had succeeded in bringing together warriors from various tribes to fight for the British. Both Brock and Tecumseh were military geniuses, and Hull was no match for them, even though his troops at Detroit outnumbered the British and their Indian allies almost two to one. Tecumseh commanded only 600 warriors, but he fooled Hull into thinking there were many more by parading them within the general's sight on three different occasions.

The British set up guns to fire at the fort, and Tecumseh's men surrounded it. Because some members of General Hull's family were inside the fort, he had nightmares about their safety, dreaming that his grandchildren's scalps were hanging from Tecumseh's lodge. Every day Hull became more and more frightened and unsure.

THE LOSS OF DETROIT

On August 16, the British commander of the Canadian forces began a bombardment of Fort Detroit. Lydia Bacon,

*General Hull was certain of defeat and feared
for the safety of those inside Fort Detroit.*

who had been sent on to Detroit following the capture of the
U.S. ship, recorded what she saw:

> as some Ladies were making cylinders (bags to hold the
> powder) & scraping lint in case it should be wanted, a 24
> pound shot entered the next door to the one they were in,
> & cut two Officers who were standing in the entry directly
> in two their bowels gushing out, the same ball passed
> through the Wall into a room where a number of people
> were & took the legs of one man off & the flesh of the thigh
> of another.... never shall I forget my sensation as I crossed
> the Parade ground to gain the place of safty, ... I felt as if my
> nerves would burst, my hair felt as if it were erect upon my
> head, which was not covered, & my eyes raised upward to

catch a glimpse of the bombs shells & balls that were flying in all directions.[4]

Because Hull was so frightened and certain of defeat, he lost his ability to command. He raised the white flag and became the first and only American officer to surrender an American city to a foreign power.

The officers and their men were outraged. They had not been consulted about the surrender, and they knew they had plenty of ammunition and sufficient forces to ward off the attack. Losing Detroit and the army there was devastating to the morale of the U.S. forces. Naturally, it had the opposite effect on the other side. When the Indians saw the weakness of the Americans, more and more tribes joined the British cause. Throughout the west, settlements were harassed.

THE DEATH OF TECUMSEH

The fortunes of the British were on the rise until General Brock was killed leading his troops in a battle at Niagara in October 1812. Colonel Henry Procter, a British military leader as timid as the American General Hull, took Brock's place.

The British controlled Detroit and had established a fort on the Raisin River in American territory. In January 1813, an American army advancing toward Detroit was defeated at Frenchtown. The British left the American wounded to the mercy of the Indians, who massacred them all. The slogan "remember the Raisin" became a rallying cry for American troops.

Colonel Procter decided to abandon the effort to hold Detroit when he learned that General William Henry Harrison, a hero of the battle at Tippecanoe River, was in command of U.S. western forces.

Harrison's appointment meant a lot to the U.S. soldiers in the field, as is evident from the journal entry of Elias Darnall, a young Kentucky volunteer:

> Gen Harrison arrived here with about one hundred mounted troops, and two days ration of flour. We have been without bread four days.—We were informed Gen. Harrison was appointed commander in chief of the North-Western-Army; this was pleasing news to the troops, as he was their choice in preference to any other.[5]

Harrison's plan was to recapture Detroit. He organized a large force from the western frontier and started moving north. The British redcoats were unable to stop the U.S. Army's advance at Fort Meigs on Lake Erie, so Colonel Procter decided to pull his men out of Detroit and move back across the water to the Canadian side at Fort Malden. Then he ordered his men to pack up and head farther east, a move that disgusted Tecumseh. The Shawnee chief tried to shame the British commander into making a stand:

> You always told us you would never draw your foot off British ground; but now, father, we see that you are drawing back.…We must compare our Father's conduct to a fat animal, that carries its tail upon its back, but when afrighted, he drops it between his legs and runs off.[6]

Harrison caught up to the retreating armies on October 5, 1813, at the Thames River in Canada. He ordered his men into the British lines, and the redcoats scattered. Indian warriors under Tecumseh came out of the swamps and attacked the American troops. Hand-to-hand combat continued until Tecumseh was slain and the Indians retreated. The Americans could once again claim most of the regions they had controlled at the outbreak of the war more than a year before.

SOME WINS, MORE LOSSES

In addition to Harrison's gains, there had been another major American victory just a month earlier, September 10, on the Great Lakes. The fearless and renowned Commodore Oliver Hazard Perry, who had been at sea since he was

Tecumseh was killed in a battle against American forces led by General Harrison. After his death, the league of Indian tribes allied to the British broke up.

eleven, was sent to break a British blockade. The blockade prevented American ships from getting out of a bay onto Lake Erie. Because Perry had a small crew, he called for reinforcements from Commodore Isaac Chauncey, who was defending Lake Ontario.

When Chauncey sent several black seamen, Perry complained at first. But Chauncey told Perry that "the colour of the skin . . . [and] the cut and trimmings of the coat" have nothing to do with "a man's qualifications or usefulness. I have nearly fifty blacks on board [my] ship, and many of them are among my best men."[7]

Perry later had high praise for his black crew members, who performed admirably, as did most other black sailors, who made up about 15 percent of American seamen at that time. With his crew, Perry led a fleet of two flagships and several smaller gunboats in the now famous Battle of Lake Erie. During the battle, Perry's ship was nearly destroyed, but he jumped into a smaller craft, went after one of the British ships, boarded it, and took control. Then he led the American fleet into a fierce and deadly exchange that defeated the British. Later, in a report to Harrison, he scribbled words that have been repeated in many battles since: "We have met the enemy and they are ours."

In spite of such victories against major odds, the history of the Canadian campaign could hardly be called a success for the U.S. forces. Many ordinary people sacrificed everything to serve in the militia and regular army regiments that traveled hundreds of miles under extremely difficult conditions to do combat. But because of poor preparation, inept leadership, and a scarcity of supplies and food, the U.S. troops could never take advantage of their superior numbers and their close proximity to the western frontier.

Young and old alike fell in battle. One elderly soldier was able to leave a final word about the deadly consequences of the war on the frontier. He scribbled a note on a scrap of paper and placed it in a bottle, which he anchored in a tree hollow. More than a century later, a farmer in Miami County, Indiana, cut down the decaying tree and found the bottle inside the stump. The faded note dated December 20, 1812, was still inside. It read:

> I am now 61. Am lost in the fight with General Harrison and was lost in the fight at Fort Tippecanoe. I am wounded in the lung and will die soon. I will put this letter in this tree for someone to find and remember me. I will now leave a wife and three children.
>
> Ever yours,
> Ben Martin.[8]

Five

✦

WAR ON THE SEA

$\mathcal{A}$t the outbreak of the war, the United States had only sixteen ships ready to defend its shores. The British, in contrast, had more than 600 ships, and they dominated all of the world's important oceans. Since battle on the high seas with the British was out of the question, the small U.S. Navy planned to concentrate its defensive efforts on the harbors and strategic shoreline installations along the Atlantic.

During the war, a number of naval battles were fought so close to shore that crowds gathered to watch. A Boston schoolteacher recorded in her diary that she joined spectators atop a hill to observe one early encounter between U.S. and British frigates:

> At 4 minutes before 6 the action commenced and in a few minutes they appeared to be yard arm to yard arm When both ships were enveloped in smoke. In about 15 minutes they separated & stood to the eastward . . . a terrible explosion took place on board the [U.S. frigate] and when the smoke cleared away the British colors were seen flying over the American.[1]

No one anywhere thought that the small, inexperienced U.S. naval force would stand a chance against the established

This 1812 drawing shows the capture of British brigs Detroit *(9) and* Caledonia *(10) during a naval battle on Lake Erie.*

British navy. But then, no one figured on the American officers being as courageous and determined as they would prove to be. Many were like Isaac Hull, the nephew of General William Hull.

Unlike his uncle, the younger Hull was not an embarrassment to the U.S. government. Instead, he proved to be a superb and brave tactician and was able to claim the first real victory over the British at the start of the war.

Isaac Hull had been sailing in the navy since the age of fourteen and became commander of a small ship at nineteen. By the time war was declared, he had seen a great deal of action, fighting pirates in the Caribbean Sea and off the coast of North Africa. Just hours after hostilities began, President Madison ordered the frigate *Constitution* into service at New York Harbor to defend against a suspected attack by British ships in the region. Hull was assigned to captain the frigate.

Because the U.S. naval force was so small, captains had been ordered to avoid confrontations with the British whenever possible. However, Captain Hull, like other American sailors, had been abused for years by the bullying tactics of the British navy. Isaac Hull meant to set the record straight. When he left dock at Annapolis, Maryland, to sail to New York, he and his men were ready to prove themselves.

CAT AND MOUSE

On board for that passage was the ship's surgeon, Amos A. Evans, who maintained a log of each day's activities. His entry of July 17, 1812, told of the start of an adventure that would spark the fire of patriotism in Americans back on shore. He wrote, "At 5 A.M. discovered another sail astern, making 2 Frigates off our Lee quarter, and 2 frigates and one ship of the line, one brig and one schooner astern, with English colours hoisted."[2]

Hull had sighted the heavily armed squadron of five British vessels and decided to make a run for shore. Besides the fact that the Americans were greatly outnumbered, there was no wind. He decided on some unusual maneuvers. First he sent small boats out front to pull the frigate along by rowing and positioned guns at the rear to fire on the pursuing ships, then he started the desperate run toward a safe haven. Captain Hull soon discovered that his ship was in very shallow water, so he ordered his men to toss out the small boats' anchors a distance ahead, then pull toward them hand over hand on the ropes. In this manner, the crew inched the *Constitution* forward, hour after hour.

The British ships matched Hull's maneuvers, and the chase continued all through the day and into the next. By the end of the second day, Hull finally was able to pilot his ship into Boston Harbor. Word of his brilliant feat spread quickly, and the British themselves had to admit that his actions were extraordinary.

Captain Hull was not finished. After taking on supplies, he went back out to sea without awaiting further orders. On August 19, 1812, the *Constitution* came upon one of the British fleet's finest specimens, HMS *Guerrière*. In his log entry for that day, Amos Evans wrote:

> We stood towards her [the *Guerrière*] with reefed topsails without shewing our colours. She then commenced firing, and gave us several broadsides without much effect before we commenced firing. . . . We hoisted our colours and fired the first gun about 15 minutes past 5 o'clock P.M., but did not come into close action until about 6 o'clock.[3]

Captain Hull himself reported that the *Constitution*'s guns destroyed the masts and knocked out most of the crew. "In less than thirty minutes, from the time we got alongside of the Enemy, she was left without a Spar Standing, and the Hull cut to pieces, in such a manner as to make it difficult to keep her above water."[4] After the crew was taken off the *Guerrière*, it was set ablaze. The Americans had shown they could fight the good fight against the all-powerful British navy.

To this day, the *Constitution* is one of America's most famous vessels. Many know the ship as Old Ironsides, a nickname it earned when a sailor on the sturdy frigate saw a cannonball bounce off its side during the battle. He yelled out that "her sides are made of iron."

Captain Isaac Hull

PRIVATEERS

During the War of 1812, as in the Revolutionary War, both the U.S. and British governments used privately owned ships for warfare. In fact, because the U.S. navy was so small, the federal government relied on privateers, which were outfitted with guns and given a commission to sail under the country's flag. Within the first six months of the War of 1812, U.S. privateers captured 450 British prizes—the ships and the goods they were carrying.

Frequently, when a ship was captured, there were casualties on both sides. In one encounter, William Paul, a young British seafarer from Nova Scotia, was killed in a fight with an American privateer. Paul's wife, Almira, at home in Halifax, was left with two young children to support. She needed to find a means of income, and she also wanted revenge for the death of her husband, who "had fallen by the hands of the Americans. I conceived them alone the authors of my misery," she declared.

In desperation, Almira left her children with her mother, disguised herself in her husband's clothes, and hired out as a cook's mate on a British cutter. On her first voyage, she witnessed the battle between the *Guerrière* and the *Constitution.* "O, it was indeed a mortifying sight . . . to see the complete distruction of one of his majesty's best frigates. . . . From this moment I began to . . . despair of very soon meeting with an opportunity to revenge the death of my husband," she wrote in a journal.[5]

For three years, Almira served without anyone discovering her gender. During that time, she was transferred to other ships, was captured twice, and escaped both times. She also took part in the capture of an American privateer. While on British ships, Almira continued her duties as a cook's mate, but in one tour of duty had to serve with a "vile, malicious and inhuman" chief cook who beat her for the slightest mistake. In retaliation, she kicked the chief cook overboard one day, and was flogged in punishment. Still, Almira recorded in her journal that she was "pleased to think to what length a female might carry her adventures, what hardships she could endure and what dangers brave, and all without betraying her sex!"[6]

Whatever Almira's accomplishments as a British sailor, there was little doubt that England suffered tremendous losses on the seas, mainly in the waters around Canada and in the Caribbean. British politicians and newspaper editorials bemoaned the fact that while the British navy had rarely lost a battle to the French fleet, ships were being burned and taken every day by the upstarts in the New World. These successes gave a much needed boost to American morale. Many who were discouraged because of the Canadian campaign now gained new hope that the U.S. cause could be won.

However, the situation in Europe was about to change dramatically. Napoleon's army was defeated in Russia. England would no longer have to support two wars, and could now concentrate on the United States.

Six

★

THE BOMBS BURSTING IN AIR

The British were ready for revenge. They had had enough of the Americans attacking and destroying their mighty navy, and they had heard of the burning and sacking of Canadian towns by renegade U.S. militiamen. Now that Napoleon and the French were out of the picture, the full weight of the British military could be thrown at the former colonies. The British war council decided that Washington, D.C., should be the first target of the new campaign.

Vice-Admiral Sir Alexander Cochrane commanded a fleet of more than forty ships and 4,500 troops on a mission to capture and destroy the nation's capital. The disciplined redcoats met only a disorganized, ragtag mix of unprepared militia. In the view of one British officer on the scene, the Americans "seemed [like] country people, who would have been much more appropriately employed in attending to their agricultural occupations, than in standing, with their muskets in their hands."[1] Slight resistance at the outset turned into a rout, with the American troops running until they were fully 16 miles (26 kilometers) from Washington.

THE CAPITAL FALLS

The Americans had expected the English to attack Baltimore first, so most defenses were sent there, leaving Washington almost totally undefended. President Madison received a letter from his secretary of state, James Monroe, on August 23, 1814, warning, "The enemy has advanced six miles along the road to the wood-yard, and our troops are retreating. You had better make all preparations to leave."[2]

The president gathered the important government papers and fled into the surrounding countryside to try to keep the government functioning. His wife, Dolley, stayed to prepare for the British onslaught at the White House. Her niece wrote of the panic that followed:

> Scarcely had the wagons that bore the papers crossed the wooden bridge over the Potomac, than crowds of fugitive women and children pressed upon it, in such numbers as to render the present danger even greater than the one they were fleeing from. The frightened multitude swayed to and fro, seeking means of escape, till night closed in upon the horrible drama; then upon Capitol Hill, appeared the red-coated soldiery of the British army.[3]

The raiders immediately fired on the Capitol building and then set out through the deserted town to find the White House. The First Lady's niece reported that "Mrs. Madison lingered on at the President's house for Mr. Madison's return, until the British officers were actually at the threshold. . . . She had secured the Declaration of Independence, and was being hurried out to the waiting carriage . . . when her eye was attracted by the valuable portrait of General Washington hanging on the wall. . . . She felt she could not leave it."[4] The picture had "to be unscrewed from the wall," as Dolley Madison herself wrote at the time, explaining:

> This process was found too tedious for these perilous moments; I have ordered the frame to be broken, and the

canvas taken out. It is done! and the precious portrait placed in the hands of two gentlemen from New York for safe keeping. And now . . . I must leave this house, or the retreating army will take me a prisoner.[5]

The First Lady did make her escape, but she was turned away from the door of two homes where she sought refuge because the families blamed President Madison for the terrible destruction that was now going on all around them. The city continued to burn throughout the night, with the glow from the fire visible as far away as Philadelphia. The British troops left for their ships in triumph the next day. Morale was as low as it could be in the United States.

The British burning the Library of Congress in 1814

THE BALTIMORE CAMPAIGN

Confident that the American resistance was almost over, Vice-Admiral Cochrane directed his forces at his second target: the city of Baltimore. While seasoned British general Robert Ross brought his soldiers overland to engage the city's defenders, the British navy sailed up the Chesapeake Bay toward Baltimore's harbor.

This time the Americans were prepared. Some 16,000 troops were deployed in the city's defense, along with hundreds of citizen volunteers. Scores of boats were deliberately sunk at the entrance of the harbor just south of Fort McHenry, the main point of defense for the city. When the British attacked at North Point, southeast of Baltimore, on September 12, 1814, the resistance of the Maryland militia was fierce. The Americans eventually forced the British land forces to retreat.

The Royal Navy was having a rough passage, too. Because of the barricade, heavy ships could not navigate the harbor, so Cochrane was forced to bring in rocket ships, directing the big guns at Fort McHenry. He hoped to knock out the guns of the fort and to silence the thousand-man force there. Then smaller ships could snake their way into the harbor and bombard Baltimore. One witness of this attack on the fort was Francis Scott Key.

DAWN'S EARLY LIGHT

Key was a young lawyer who had come from his home in Washington with an artillery militia to defend Baltimore. He was asked to negotiate the release of Doctor William Beanes, who was being held on a British warship under the command of Vice-Admiral Cochrane. The old doctor had been caught resisting the British advance on the Capitol, and his friends were concerned about his condition.

With John S. Skinner, a federal government agent, Key boarded a U.S. ship that carried a flag of truce and was being used by American officials attempting to negotiate with the British. Key and Skinner reached the British warship just as it was about to attack. The two men won the release of the physician, but the British would not let the Americans return to shore where they could inform patriots of the planned attack on Fort McHenry. So they held all three men on the truce ship behind the British fleet as Cochrane ordered the bombing of the fort to begin.

Throughout the day and night of September 13, up to two thousand cannonballs were shot into the fort. From his vantage point on the truce boat, Francis Key kept his telescope trained on the huge flag flying over the fort. Every time the doctor asked him about the flag, Key would assure him that it was still there. And in the early hours of first light on the next day, all of Baltimore could see that the shelling had failed to dislodge the defenders.

Cochrane had to give up the attack and withdraw his navy and army back down the Chesapeake. The English plan to invade and destroy the mid-Atlantic region had only been partially successful. Although the destruction of Washington had been devastating to the United States, the defense of Baltimore bolstered the spirits of a very worried country.

Francis Scott Key helped to provide a rallying cry with the creation of the song he wrote the day after he witnessed the attack on Fort McHenry. Set to the tune of a popular drinking song, Key's inspiring words were printed soon after the battle under the title "Defence of Fort M'Henry." And the publisher included this introduction:

He [Key] watched the flag at the Fort through the whole day with an anxiety that can be better felt than described, until the night prevented him from seeing it. In the night he

This giant flag—originally fifty feet long—flew over
Fort McHenry when the British attacked the fort in September 1814.

watched the bomb shells, and at early dawn his eye was
again greeted by the proudly waving flag of his country.[6]

Two years later, the song was published as "The Star-
Spangled Banner." In 1931, it became the official national
anthem of the United States.

Seven

A PROUD VICTORY

Even with the great defense of Baltimore, most Americans realized that their country was in jeopardy. The federal government was nearly bankrupt. There was hardly enough money in the coffers to pay for the soldiers and sailors out on the lines. Certainly there was not enough money to pay for the additional recruits who were desperately needed to succeed on the final front of the war: the South. This area was the least populated and most poorly defended of any in the settled United States.

Knowing his advantage, Vice-Admiral Cochrane led his troops toward the Gulf of Mexico. The English also knew that they had an ally in the South: Creek Indian Chief Red Eagle (or William Weatherford, as he was known to his Scottish father). Red Eagle had heard Tecumseh's message when the Shawnee chief had traveled among the southern nations the previous year. While most Creeks had stayed neutral at the outbreak of the war between the United States and England, Red Eagle and his men had not. In August 1813, they had staged a raid against Fort Mims, an American settlers' outpost on the Alabama River in Mississippi Territory.

There had been few threats from Indian tribes in that area, so the troops located at Fort Mims had grown comfortably secure. The soldiers and the five hundred settlers under their protection were caught totally off guard when the Creeks attacked, torching many buildings and killing all but thirty-five of the settlers as they ran screaming from the flames. The government responded quickly by authorizing 3,500 troops and $300,000 to put down the uprising.

Among the men assigned to track down the warring Creeks was Lieutenant Joseph Willcox, a young West Point graduate. In letters to his father in Connecticut, Willcox reported on the action he saw in the hostile frontier of the South. On December 6, 1813, he wrote that

> the British had landed a large body of troops at Pensacola ... [and] have offered to furnish the Spaniards with 2,000 black troops, for the defence of Pensacola. The Spaniards have lately furnished the Creek Indians with powder and other munitions of war.... I expect the seat of the war to be in this part of the country, and that we shall have a bloody scene. ...We expect to see some of the enemy shortly. [1]

The Creek Indians massacred several hundred settlers at Fort Mims.

Three weeks later, he followed up with this message:

> I have but just time to say, that we succeeded in burning Echanachaca, (or Beloved Ground) which was one of the principal towns of deposit for corn and treasure in the Creek nation. The Indians heard of our approach only in time to get their women and children across the river, when we attacked them. The town was defended by 120 Indians and Negroes (the latter the most desperate foe.) . . . We killed 30 of them, and had one killed and 5 wounded. [2]

Not long after writing that letter, Lieutenant Willcox was ordered to take three men and row downriver to warn another group of soldiers to stay where they were camped. After traveling at least 120 miles (193 kilometers), capsizing once, going without provisions many days, and avoiding the fire of some pursuing warriors, they were attacked by eight Creeks in a canoe. Walter Bourke, a friend of Lieutenant Willcox, described the sad outcome of that mission in a letter dated January 19, 1814, which he sent to his comrade's father:

> My Dear Sir—No doubt you will be surprized at the familiar style in which an utter stranger addresses you. . . . Great God! what an excruciating task to perform! Where should I find the language to convey as I could wish, by stealth, into the bosom of an amiable family, the sorrowful tidings of the premature fall of a favorite son! [3]

BATTLING THE CREEKS

Andrew Jackson was placed in charge of the force in which Lieutenant Willcox fought and died. Jackson was a tough and independent officer. When he was assigned to lead the large southern army, he was recuperating from wounds suffered in a duel just days before.

Even with the poor state of Jackson's health, he got his men moving just nine days later, traveling at the rate of 20 miles (32 kilometers) per day, a fast pace for that part of the country and the rough terrain. They moved in the direction of the Creeks' stronghold, first catching them at the village of Tallushatchee. There, the outnumbered warriors were "shot like dogs," according to young Davy Crockett, who was among the troops that day.

Red Eagle was just 30 miles (48 kilometers) away, and Jackson rushed to find him. Arriving at Talladega, the American troops were attacked by Creeks descending "like a cloud of Egyptian locusts," according to Crockett, "and screaming like all the young devils had been turned loose, with the old devil of all at their head."[4] Jackson's army mowed them down in rapid-fire succession. The battle lasted only fifteen minutes, and almost 400 Indians were killed.

On March 27, 1814, the final Creek battle was fought when 2,000 Americans faced off against 900 of Red Eagle's men at Horseshoe Bend. Jackson ordered a full-out assault against the front of the Creek barricades. For hours the battle raged, and by the time it was over at least 500 more Creeks were dead. Their resistance was crushed.

Several days following the battle, a starving, wretched Red Eagle walked into the American camp alone. He found General Jackson and said:

> I am Bill Weatherford. I am in your power, do with me as you please. I am a soldier. I have done the white people all the harm I could; I have fought them, and fought them bravely; if I had an army, I would yet fight, and contend to the last: but I have none; my people are all gone. I can do no more than weep over the misfortunes of my nation.[5]

Andrew Jackson was so impressed by the Creek leader's honor and attitude that he released him. Bill Weatherford (Red Eagle) never fought against the Americans again. For all practical purposes, the Indian uprising in the South was over. But the British continued to arm the tribes wherever they thought it would be advantageous.

THE "RAG-TAG" ARMY

By the end of 1814, reports were circulating that the British navy was assembling off the coast of Pensacola, Florida. The English forces were huge in number, and the only real

Creek Chief Red Eagle surrendered to General Andrew Jackson after the Indians were defeated at Horseshoe Bend in Alabama.

defense for Americans in that region was Andrew Jackson's "little army."

In early December, Jackson arrived in New Orleans to help fortify the city against the expected British attack. He had only about 2,000 men, who were immediately put to work building barricades and positioning themselves as best they could. Jackson organized other troops of volunteer soldiers among local residents.

As it is today, New Orleans was a culturally diverse city in the 1800s. It had been a Spanish territory as well as a French possession prior to its passing to the United States in the Louisiana Purchase of 1803. People of varied ancestries called the area their home, and the local militia reflected that diversity. Jackson put together a force that was described by one historian as a "bobtailed, rag-tagged, motley collection of Tennessee sharpshooters, Mississippi Dragoons, Kentucky riflemen, Choctaw Indians, Negro slaves and free men of color, Louisiana Creoles and Cajuns, Irishmen, Germans and Jews, and renegade privateersmen and pirates."[6]

Using free men of color and slaves as infantrymen was not something the nation accepted easily. There was widespread fear that armed slaves would take the earliest opportunity to turn on their masters and massacre as many whites as they could. But Martin Delany, a black abolitionist and journalist of the time, noted that blacks were as willing to fight for the United States as any others. They were "not compelled to go; they were not draughted [drafted]. They were volunteers," Delany wrote.[7]

The governor of Louisiana, W.C.C. Claiborne, also had been advocating the enlistment of blacks for over a decade. He wrote to General Jackson: "These men, Sir, for the most part sustain good characters. Many of them have extensive connections and much property to defend, and all seem attached to arms. . . . If we give them not our confidence, the enemy will be encouraged to intrigue and corrupt them."[8]

Indeed, the governor had heard reports of some free blacks taking the side of the Spaniards, who were allies of the British. And the British, as they did during the Revolutionary War, offered freedom to slaves who joined their forces. Claiborne was convinced that the government should allow these men to fight for their country or they might fight against it.

THE UNLIKELY VICTORY

On December 23, 1814, the British captured a plantation just south of New Orleans. They planned to launch an attack the next day to capture the city. Jackson knew that the British would bring in reinforcements, so he prepared American soldiers for a major advance. An additional force of some 2,500 Tennessee reinforcements arrived just as the British started toward New Orleans.

Among the Americans were two black regiments and a drummer boy of biracial ancestry, Jordan Noble, who later became famous for his bravery. With the roll of his drum, fourteen-year-old Jordan helped guide soldiers through darkness and a dense fog, while fierce fighting raged around him.

In a series of clashes over nearly three weeks, the British soldiers and the tenacious troops of Andrew Jackson traded fire, positions, cannonballs, and blood. Then, on January 8, 1815, Sir Edward Pakenham, a British general, ordered a full frontal assault on the American lines. He sent row after row of his men at the four lines of Jackson's sharpshooters.

Since the Americans were heavily outnumbered, Pakenham was certain that his men would overrun Jackson's troops. But it never happened. As one British officer some distance from the actual fighting said, "These d——d Yankee riflemen can pick a squirrel's eye out as far as they can see it."[9] The redcoats were hit with a steady volley of musket shot that killed or wounded 2,000 men, sending the remaining troops back to their ships in the Gulf.

As the news spread about Jackson's victory at New Orleans, newspaper editorials and politicians praised the feat with words like "brilliant," "glorious," and "splendid." Americans expected to go on to win many more battles and end the war, but strangely enough, peace already had been declared.

Both American and British officials had been trying to negotiate peace all through the years of the war. Two weeks before the New Orleans victory, on December 24, 1814, they had finally signed a treaty in Ghent, a town in Belgium. But because of the slow means of communication, word of the treaty did not reach the United States until the middle of February 1815.

A newspaper clipping announcing the signing of the peace treaty officially ending the War of 1812

THE AFTERMATH

News of the peace treaty was also slow to reach American prisoners of war who were held in an infamous prison compound known as Dartmoor, located in a desolate, foggy, and cold area of England. The prison compound was made up of two-story stone buildings and housed thousands of U.S. seamen as well as some British deserters and French prisoners who had been captured on the high seas. Because of unhealthy conditions inside the dark, dank buildings, many prisoners suffered from pneumonia and smallpox, which were responsible for hundreds of deaths.

Most of the Americans in Dartmoor were sailors from port cities in the United States. In late March 1815, when American prisoners heard about the end of the war, they reacted with great joy and naturally were anxious to be released. U.S. officials, however, were slow to send ships for the prisoners' return, and tension began to rise in the compound.

On April 6, some prisoners, looking for diversion, began to chip away at loose stones in an inner wall that separated each section from the walled courtyard. Although chiseling at the wall was not an escape attempt, the guards fired on the prisoners, killing or wounding more than thirty. Of the seven who died, one was a fourteen-year-old.

Because of the massacre, Dartmoor prison gained a notorious reputation. But after the tragedy, both the United States and Britain supplied vessels to repatriate American prisoners, and by June most of the Americans had returned home.

Meantime, on the home front, Americans had been celebrating for months with parades, bonfires, band concerts, political speeches, church services, community singing, and many other events. Once again people in the United States had successfully resisted British attempts to dominate.

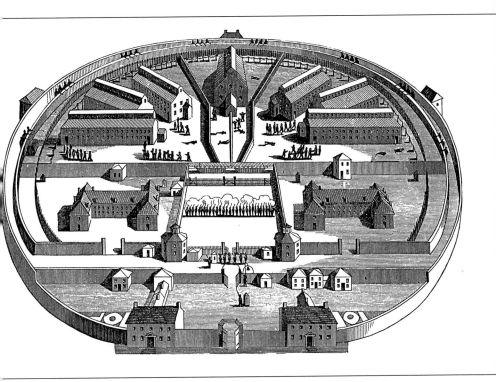

Dartmoor prison in England housed thousands of U.S. seamen
who had been captured during the war.

With the end of the war, the British finally acknowledged that the people of the United States were citizens of a separate country, not rebellious British subjects. Americans gained new national heroes, among them Andrew Jackson, who later became president of the United States. Many also felt a sense of identity and pride in their nation. As one enthusiastic North Carolinian observed, "I think the war . . . has shewn the world that a set of free men under a free government contending for their rights and privilidges against a set of tyrants and despots are invincible."[10]

Source Notes

One

1. Jacob B. Varnum, *Journal of Jacob B. Varnum of Petersburg, Virginia* (1864; typed copy of original, Chicago: Chicago Historical Society Museum Library).

2. Quoted in Robert M. Utley and Wilcomb E. Washburn, *The American Heritage History of the Indian Wars* (New York: American Heritage Publishing Co. and Bonanza Books, 1982), 122.

3. Ibid, 133.

4. Ibid.

5. Quoted in Wesley J. Whickar, "Shabonee's Account of Tippecanoe," *Indiana Magazine of History,* December 1921, 357.

6. John Tipton, *Journal of Tippecanoe Expedition, September 12–November 24, 1811* (typed copy of original, Lafayette, Ind.: Tippecanoe County Historical Association Library).

7. Ibid.

Two

1. Benjamin Frederick Browne, ed., *The Yarn of a Yankee Privateer Edited by Nathaniel Hawthorne* (New York: Funk and Wagnalls Company, 1926), 66–67.

2. John M'Lean, *Seventeen Years' History, of the Life and Sufferings of James M'Lean, an Impressed American Citizen and Seaman, Embracing But a Summary of What He Endured, While Detained in the British Service, during That Long and Painful Period, "Written by Himself"* (Hartford, Conn.: B. and J. Russell, 1814, Lilly Library, Indiana University, Bloomington, Ind.), 7.

3. Ibid, 10.

4. Quoted in Donald R. Hickey, *The War of 1812: A Forgotten Conflict* (Urbana, Ill.: University of Illinois Press, 1989), 26.

Three

1. Quoted in Hickey, *War of 1812*, 54–55.
2. Ibid, 55.
3. Ibid, 59.
4. Ibid, 66.
5. Elias Darnall, *A Journal and Two Narratives* (New York: Garland Publishing, 1978), 28–29.

Four

1. William Hull to Charles Scott, May 12, 1812, Lilly Library.
2. Mary M. Crawford, ed., "Mrs. Lydia B. Bacon's Journal, 1811–1812," *Indiana Magazine of History*, December 1944, 66–67.
3. Quoted in Hickey, *War of 1812*, 81.
4. Ibid, 71.
5. Darnall, *Journal and Two Narratives*, 17–18.
6. Utley and Washburn, *Indian Wars*, 138.
7. Quoted in Reginald Horsman, "The Paradox of Dartmoor Prison," *American Heritage*, February 1975, 14.
8. Ben Martin, December 20, 1812, Chicago Historical Society Museum Library.

Five

1. Handwritten journal, January 7–September 9, 1812, Lilly Library.
2. Amos A. Evans, *Journal Kept on Board the Frigate "Constitution," 1812,* reprinted for William D. Sawtell from the *Pennsylvania Magazine of History and Biography* (Lincoln Massachusetts, 1967), 153.

3. Ibid.

4. Quoted in Hickey, *War of 1812*, 94.

5. [Almira Paul?], *The Surprising Adventures of Almira Paul, a Young Woman, who, garbed as a Male, has for three of the last preceding years, actually served as a common Sailor, on board of English and American vessels, without a discovery of her sex being made* (Boston: M. Brewster, 1816, Lilly Library), 4–11.

6. Ibid.

Six

1. Quoted in Hickey, *War of 1812*, 198.

2. Dolley Madison, *Memoirs and Letters of Dolly Madison wife of James Madison, President of the United States Edited by Her Grand-Niece* (Boston: Houghton, Mifflin and Company; Cambridge: Riverside Press, 1887), 101.

3. Ibid.

4. Ibid, 106–107.

5. Ibid, 110–111.

6. "Defence of Fort M'Henry," Lilly Library.

Seven

1. *A Narrative of the Life and Death of Lieut. Joseph Morgan Willcox, Who was Massacred by the Creek Indians, On the Alabama River, (Miss. Ter.) On the 15th of January, 1814—Compiled from various publications, and letters written By his friends and brother Officers, On the occasion.*—(Published by consent of his Friends.) (1816; reprint, New York: Garland Publishing, 1978), 5.

2. Ibid, 5–6.

3. Ibid, 7.

4. Quoted in Utley and Washburn, *Indian Wars*, 141.

5. Ibid.

6. Quoted in Marcus Christian, *Negro Soldiers in the Battle*

of New Orleans (New Orleans: Battle of New Orleans 150th Anniversary Committee of Louisiana, 1965), 24.

7. Martin R. Delany, *The Condition, Evaluation, Emigration, and Destiny of the Colored People of the United States* (New York: Arno Press, 1969), 73.

8. Quoted in Christian, *Negro Soldiers*, 14.

9. Quoted in Hickey, *War of 1812*, 212.

10. Quoted in Sarah McCulloh Lemmon, *Frustrated Patriots* (Chapel Hill, N.C.: University of North Carolina Press, 1973), 202.

Further Reading

Berton, Pierre. *The Capture of Detroit.* Buffalo, N.Y.: Firefly Books, 1992.

Bosco, Peter I. *War of 1812.* Brookfield, Conn.: Millbrook Press, 1991.

Carter, Alden R. *The War of 1812: Second Fight for Independence.* New York: Watts, 1993.

Marrin, Albert. *Eighteen Twelve: The War Nobody Won.* New York: Atheneum, 1985.

Morris, Richard B. *The War of 1812.* rev. ed. Minneapolis: Lerner, 1985.

Nardo, Don. *The War of 1812.* San Diego: Lucent, 1991.

Index